Darlene Misconish Tyler, M.Ed.

Consultant

Lorrie McConnell, M.A.
Professional Development Specialist TK–12
Moreno Valley USD, CA

Publishing Credits

Rachelle Cracchiolo, M.S.Ed., *Publisher*
Conni Medina, M.A.Ed., *Managing Editor*
Dona Herweck Rice, *Series Developer*
Emily R. Smith, M.A.Ed., *Series Developer*
Diana Kenney, M.A.Ed., NBCT, *Content Director*
June Kikuchi, *Content Director*
Stacy Monsman, M.A., *Editor*
Michelle Jovin, M.A., *Assistant Editor*
Fabiola Sepulveda, *Graphic Designer*

Image Credits: p.5 Edward Parker/Alamy; p.6 left Granger, NYC; pp.7 bottom, 11 bottom, 13 Cornell Capa/The Life Picture Collection/Getty Images; p.8 Bettmann/Getty Images; p.9 Felix Choo/Alamy; p.10 left studiomode/Alamy; p.11 top Borthwick Institute Heritage Images/Newscom; pp.14, 15 winhorse/iStock; p.16 Chip East/Reuters/Newscom; p.17 Jochen Tack/ImageBroker/Newscom; all other images from iStock and/or Shutterstock.

Library of Congress Cataloging-in-Publication Data

Names: Tyler, Darlene Misconish, author.
Title: Your world : bubblegum / Darlene Misconish Tyler.
Other titles: Bubblegum
Description: Huntington Beach, CA : Teacher Created Materials, [2018] | Audience: K to grade 3. | Includes index. |
Identifiers: LCCN 2017049088 (print) | LCCN 2018002119 (ebook) | ISBN 9781480759961 (eBook) | ISBN 9781425857462 (pbk.)
Subjects: LCSH: Bubble gum--Juvenile literature. | Chewing gum--Juvenile literature.
Classification: LCC TX799 (ebook) | LCC TX799 .T95 2018 (print) | DDC 641.3/38--dc23
LC record available at https://lccn.loc.gov/2017049088

Teacher Created Materials
5301 Oceanus Drive
Huntington Beach, CA 92649-1030
http://www.tcmpub.com

ISBN 978-1-4258-5746-2

Printed by: 51497
Printed in: China

Table of Contents

Pop!

Chomp! Chomp! Pop! Chewing gum has been around for thousands of years. But bubblegum has a more recent history. Many people think bubblegum and chewing gum are the same thing. In fact, they are quite different.

Chewing gum is made with **sap** from trees. The sap makes the gum very chewy. Bubblegum is stretchy, which lets people blow bubbles. Some people chew it because they like the taste. Some people think it just makes a mess! Regardless of whether you are a fan, one thing is certain: bubblegum has come a long way over the years.

This man taps into the tree to get sap.

Walter's Wonder

In the early 1900s, chewing gum was sold in most stores. Many people liked the treat. But gum was sticky—very sticky. It stuck to people's hands and clothes. It even stuck to their lips!

Workers at the Fleer Corporation were trying to find a way to make a great piece of gum. A man named Walter Diemer (DEE-muhr) worked in the office there. He was not an inventor. But Walter still wanted to help. He worked for more than a year on new gum **recipes**. One day, he made the perfect **batch**. The gum was not too sticky, and it could stretch more than the old gum.

A worker feeds stretched bubblegum through a machine to flatten it.

A girl blows a giant bubble in 1959.

Bubble Blowers

Gilbert Mustin was in charge of Fleer. He called the new gum Dubble Bubble®. Before that, no one had ever blown a bubble with gum! This was a new idea. In fact, Walter had to teach sales people how to blow bubbles so they could sell the gum.

People loved Dubble Bubble. It was not sticky like the old gum. And now, they could blow huge bubbles! Other companies copied Walter's gum recipe. Within a few years, there were many brands of gum from which to choose.

LET'S EXPLORE MATH

The Fleer Corporation grew very fast because of Dubble Bubble. Walter had to teach more and more sales people how to blow bubbles. Suppose that the ten frames show how many people Walter taught on Monday and Tuesday.

Monday

•	•	•	•	•
•	•	•		

Tuesday

•	•	•	•	•
•				

1. How many people did Walter teach each day?
2. On which day did Walter teach the most people?
3. How many people did Walter teach altogether?
4. How many more people did Walter teach on Monday than on Tuesday?

Dubble Bubble gum packs come with comics.

Why Pink?

Today, most pieces of bubblegum are pink. We owe that to Walter, too. When he made his final batch of gum, he looked for a way to make it stand out. Walter grabbed a bottle of food coloring, which is a liquid that **dyes** things certain colors. The only bottle he could find was pink. Walter did not mind. His favorite color was pink! When other companies made their gum, they used pink, too.

Two workers check their gum recipe in 1935.

A factory worker mixes food coloring into a batch of bubblegum in 1947.

Love It or Hate It

Good gum used to be hard to find. But now, it is sold in most countries. People love to chomp on this chewy treat. A typical American chews about a pound of gum each year. That may seem like a lot. But around the world, more than one hundred thousand tons of gum are chewed each year. All that gum weighs about as much as 20,000 elephants! That is a lot of gum!

LET'S EXPLORE MATH

Imagine you work at a candy store. You keep track of how much chewing gum you sell.

1. In one week, you sell 4 packs of gum each day for 4 days. How many packs of gum do you sell? Explain your strategy for finding the solution using words, numbers, or pictures.
2. The next week, your goal is to sell 20 packs of gum. How many more packs is this than the first week?

Kids push in line to buy bubblegum in 1947.

Not everyone is a fan of bubblegum. In 1987, a new **metro** system was built in Singapore. Gum chewers left bits of gum on the seats and on the doors of the trains. This made the country's leaders mad. So, they wrote a law that **banned** the sale of gum. Today, only gum that is used to keep teeth clean can be sold there. But buyers must sign their names and show identification cards first.

LET'S EXPLORE MATH

Some people spit gum on the ground or stick it under tables when they are done chewing. It costs about 3¢ to make a stick of gum but 10¢ to clean it up.

1. How much more does it cost to clean up 1 piece of gum than it does to make 1 stick of gum?
2. Which costs more: cleaning up 2 pieces of gum or making 6 sticks of gum? By how much?

Singapore Metro

A man measures a girl's bubble in a contest.

Bubblegum Fun!

Love it or hate it, bubblegum is here to stay. Many people try to see who can blow the biggest bubble. Bubblegum contests are held each year at state fairs and schools. The world record was set in 2004. It was 20 inches (51 centimeters) wide.

Many people have tried to beat the record. But so far, no one has.

LET'S EXPLORE MATH

Lucky likes to compete in bubble-blowing contests. He is practicing for a big contest next weekend.

1. Imagine that Lucky blows 4 bubbles. His bubbles are 3 inches, 6 inches, 5 inches, and 2 inches wide. What is the total of the widths of Lucky's bubbles?
2. Yesterday, Lucky blew a bubble that was 18 inches wide. Today, Lucky blows a bubble that is 10 inches smaller than the one he blew yesterday. How wide is the bubble he blows today?

A group of people try to blow the biggest bubble.

Bubblegum can be fun. But it can also help you in ways that you may not realize.

Have you ever been hungry but have to wait for lunchtime? Try chewing a piece of gum. Chewing gum will trick your brain into thinking that you have food. It may even stop your stomach from growling until you can eat.

Do you have a test coming up? Some schools have been known to let kids chew gum during important tests. Chewing gum has been shown to help people focus.

This boy wishes lunchtime could be sooner.

LESSON 4 : PLANT LIFE CYCLE
A PLANT LIFE CYCLE
THE CHICKEN LIFE CYCLE

Chewing gum can help in a few more ways. It may stop you from crying when you cut an onion. Some people think it works because the gum flavor is stronger than the onion flavor. Other people think it makes you breathe through your mouth, not your nose. Still, other people think that it is all in your head. If you think it will stop you from crying, then you will.

Chewing sugar-free gum after meals might also keep your teeth strong. Gum causes your mouth to make more saliva, or spit. This clears out any food that is caught between your teeth. It also keeps your breath fresh!

A dentist shows her patient X-rays of his teeth.

Chewing gum can have many **benefits**. But it can also cause some problems. Picture yourself blowing a huge bubble. It keeps getting bigger and bigger. All of a sudden, the bubble pops! There is gum everywhere. It is even in your hair! What can you do?

There is one safe way to get the gum out of your hair, but it can get a little messy. Rub peanut butter on the gum. Then, wait a few minutes. The oils in the peanut butter will help the sticky gum come right out!

Luckily, gum comes out of hair. But what if you get bubblegum on your clothes? Getting gum out of clothes can be tricky, but it can be done! Fold your clothes, put them in a plastic bag, and put the bag in the freezer. After a few hours, you should be able to scrape the frozen gum right off! If you are in a hurry and do not have time to wait, rub an ice cube over the gum.

The gum on this pair of jeans should come off after a few hours in the freezer.

A Blast with Bubblegum

Once you clean up the mess, there are many ways to enjoy bubblegum. You can chew it, blow it, or pop it. Maybe you want to set a world record. Maybe you want to get rid of a bad taste in your mouth. Or, you might just chew gum for fun. No matter what you do, how you feel, or where you go, bubblegum is there to pop along with you!

Problem Solving

Bubble blowing is not the only contest for gum lovers. The Chomp Title goes to the person who chews the most pieces of bubblegum for the longest amount of time. The current Chomp Title champ is Richard Walker. He chewed 135 pieces of bubblegum for 8 hours!

Imagine that Alexis is competing in a contest at her school. She wants to hold the Chomp Title. There are three rounds. In her first round, she chews 10 pieces of gum for 4 hours. In the next round, she chews 6 pieces of gum for 4 hours. In her third round, she chews 4 pieces of gum for 4 hours. Answer the questions to summarize her chewing activity.

1. How many more pieces of gum does Alexis chew in round 1 than in round 2?

2. How many fewer pieces of gum does Alexis chew in round 3 than in round 2?

3. In which round does she chew the most pieces of gum? How do you know?

4. How many total pieces of gum does Alexis chew in all 3 rounds? Explain your strategy using words, numbers, or pictures.

5. For how many total hours does Alexis chew gum? How many hours more or less than Richard is this?

Glossary

banned—ordered people to stop using or doing something

batch—a group of things that are made at the same time

benefits—good results or effects

dyes—changes the colors of things

metro—an underground railway system

recipes—sets of instructions for making things

sap—a watery fluid that comes from inside a plant

Index

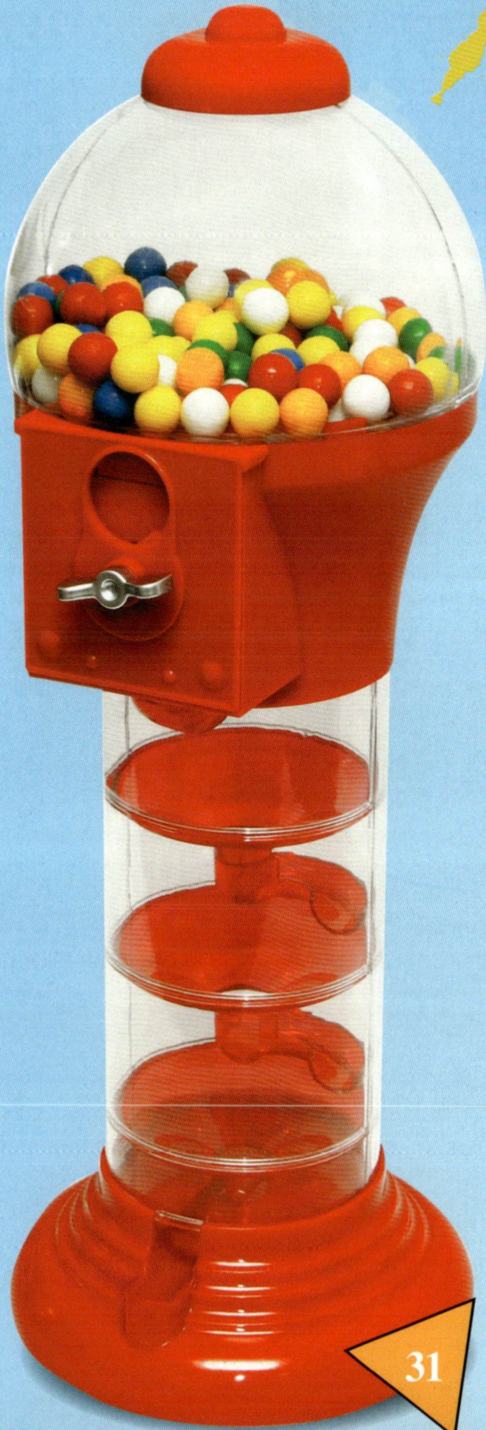

Answer Key

Let's Explore Math

page 9:

1. Monday: 8 people; Tuesday: 6 people
2. Monday
3. 14 people
4. 2 people

page 13:

1. 16 packs of gum; Strategies will vary but may include using equations, arrays, or ten frames.
2. 4 more packs of gum

page 15:

1. 7¢ more
2. Cleaning up 2 pieces of gum costs 2¢ more than making 6 sticks of gum.

page 17:

1. 16 in.
2. 8 in. wide

Problem Solving

1. 4 more pieces of gum
2. 2 fewer pieces of gum
3. round 1; Answers will vary but may include that she chewed 10 pieces in round 1, and 10 is more than 6 (round 2), and 10 is more than 4 (round 3).
4. 20 pieces of gum total; Explanations will vary but may include using equations, ten frames, or blocks.
5. Alexis chews gum for a total of 12 hours. She chews for 4 more hours than Richard.